THE DAY AMERICA CRIED!
SO MANY INNOCENTS
DIED 9-11-01

THE DAY AMERICA CRIED! SO MANY INNOCENTS DIED 9-11-01

Patricia B. Schoeler

Library of Congress Control Number:		2011914465
ISBN:	Hardcover	978-1-4653-5084-8
	Softcover	978-1-4653-5083-1
	Ebook	978-1-4653-5085-5

This book was printed in the United States of America.

To order additional copies of this book, contact:
Xlibris Corporation
1-888-795-4274
www.Xlibris.com
Orders@Xlibris.com
101550

CONTENTS

To Marie who gave me the encouragement to follow my dream and for her input, patience, and understanding as I reached my goal.

Introduction

Tuesday, September 11, 2001, started off as a typical workday in America. None of us had any idea of the destruction and devastation that was about to happen.

At 8:48 AM on this sunny, crisp September morning, our lives were irrevocably changed.

God bless those who lost their lives at the World Trade Center in New York City, the Pentagon in Washington, DC, in a field in Pennsylvania, and the passengers and crews of American Airline flight numbers 11 and 77 and United Airline flight numbers 93 and 175.

This book is a poetic history of events.

Attack on New York

What happened in New York seems so surreal
It's hard to express just how we feel

Faceless cowards strike from the sky
Begs the question of "why oh why?"

We sit watching the TV as the horrors unfold
Stories of pain and heroism are yet to be told

So many innocents have lost their lives
Loved ones left behind let out anguished cries

Visions of thousands waiting in line
Desperate for news that their loved ones are fine

Hoping against hope but knowing full well
That probably they've died in this living hell

Bands of workers forming a human chain
Working together, scenes played over again

They are heroes one, heroes all
We may be down, but we will not fall

No one in America has escaped untouched
This is a tragedy affecting us all very much

Who knew this morning that it was to be farewell
What each day brings us, there is no way to tell

Something familiar now missing from our New York skyline
The World Trade Center "magnificent," you'd hear all the time

So many lives, so much pain
Our lives can never be the same

However, we will emerge so much stronger
We won't put up with terrorism for one minute longer

Attacking our homeland is a direct violation
They've yet to learn we are a very strong nation

They cannot run, they cannot hide
For our influence is felt worldwide!
God bless America
9-12-01

Tragedies Unfold

Now heart-wrenching stories are being told
Scenarios of tragedy beginning to unfold

Desperate stories one and all
All because our Twin Towers did fall

Who really understands the meaning of fate
How some were saved because they were late

Other changes brought people *to* the building that day
Who can fathom why things happen that way?

No words can console those in pain
Because their loved ones won't be coming home again

The attack against us is senseless and vicious
Because life to Americans is wonderful and precious

Our untold gratitude to all trying to recover our dead
Horrors their eyes see, what must run through their head?

Excruciatingly slow is this job at hand
With the hours they put in, how do they still stand?

Thank you for what you are trying to do
Our love and our hearts go out to you too!
9-14-01

The Power of Unity

The power of unity is really amazing
Prayer groups are forming and candles blazing

Everyone is willing to help and to listen
To stories of pain as their own eyes glisten

The reality of this, almost too much to bear
Senseless murder, it's so unfair

We will recover from this, there is no doubt
As Americans, we are strong; it's what we are about

The strength of the human spirit fills me with awe
But it will take time because our emotions are raw

Please take comfort as the nation grieves with you
It's a common loss; we *will* all make it through!
9-15-01

There's Always Hope

Is it possible someone may still be alive?
There is always hope, so onward they strive

These men and women determined in their quest
Will not be deterred, giving beyond their best

Volunteers, we have more than enough
All areas of skills, doing their stuff

Supplies are donated in abundance you see
Everyone wants to help; this is how it's supposed to be

So many flags are flying to show our pride
Americans' patriotism will never hide!
9-15-01

Now It Begins

Now the funerals have begun
Songs of prayers are being sung

It matters not which path we choose
Because with faith, we will never lose

A common bond unites us as we kneel and pray
Our faith will carry us to begin a new day!
9-15-01

Visions

Videos and pictures continue to unfurl
Visions and sounds that make our blood curl

The evil that perpetrated this just blows my mind
This is mass murder against all mankind

Painstakingly they planned this vicious horror
They got us today, but they won't tomorrow

Watch out, terrorists, for war has been declared
As Americans, we are always prepared!
9-16-01

My Brothers

"I lost a lot of brothers this week," said with sadness in his voice
So much pain thrust on so many who had no choice

My nephew is a fireman who proudly wears his blue
Frustrated and sad because there is nothing else he can do

In the line of duty, they often risk their lives
Rushing into buildings when hearing those anguished cries

As others race out, they are trained to forge in
Facing down the danger where others had just been

A big old bear hug was all that I could do
There were no words to say, this we both knew

We'd love to erase the weariness etched on your face
Know that we all hold you in a collective warm embrace!
9-16-01

Resuming Daily Life

Trying to go back to daily life
Almost impossible amid this terrible strife

It's hard to concentrate with a heavy heart
Difficult watching our old way of life depart

No one ever thought this could happen here
To us, we hold our freedom dear

Obviously now, we must be more aware
Our liberty is at stake; we must handle with care

We will not allow them to harm us without a fight
We will work through our pain; recovery is in sight!
9-17-01

A Bucket of Pictures

A kind citizen found pictures on the street
He gathered them together, not a pleasant feat

A bucket of pictures is all that is left
Memories for families now left bereft

These pictures were released by the blast
Reminders of happy times from the past

Hopefully, they'll bring comfort in some small measure
Some tangible items to love and to treasure!
9-18-01

One Week Ago Today

What a difference a minute can make
From happy faces to instant heartbreak

The time of day was AM 8:48
September 11, 2001, was the date

That Tuesday was the day America cried
Because so may of our innocents have died!
9-18-01

Pause and Reflect

It's time for us to pause and reflect
Just what is it out of life we expect?

Take the time and get your priorities straight
There's no time like the present, no time to wait

What a lesson we are learning because our Towers fell
A difficult lesson but we have learned it well

We've learned that no one has promised us a tomorrow
Say I love you now, have no regrets along with your sorrow!
9-18-01

Such Destruction

They had to know this would start an all-out war
The likes of one we'd never seen before

Bound to be difficult and very long
Count on this fact, it will be very strong

Strategies are formulated and in the works
Due to bin Laden terrorists; that man is berserk

Without regard for human life, they're vicious and cruel
Knowing the destruction caused by aviation fuel

Attacking defenseless citizens trying to earn a living
Family members who were loving and giving

The cowards delivered us a sucker punch
Then committed suicide, the entire bunch!
9-19-01

Human Decency

These terrorists have reaped monetary gain
Off American blood and obvious pain

They trained intensely to reach their goal
Hiding among us as a virtual mole

They sneaked up behind us when our backs were turned
Knowing full well what would happen when the buildings burned

They have not one shred of human decency
They left no room to show any leniency

Don't you worry, though; we are up to the task
We will seek and find those who hide behind a coward's mask!
9-20-01

Our Guys Still at It!

These men are still going through the rubble
They feel it's their duty amid all this trouble

Working tirelessly, they never give up
Even getting hurt; those sharp edges do cut

Risking their lives every day
Looking for survivors, they hope and pray

Whether fire, police, medical, or construction
They work side by side to clean up the destruction

Only a few organizations, to name a few
Doing their best to work their way through!
9-20-01

Our Telethon

We've come together as never before
And it keeps happening more and more

A telethon ran by our biggest stars
To raise our spirits and help heal the scars

Everyone responded to answer the call
This tragedy has affected us one and all

Over two dozen channels will do simulcast
To raise money for victims of last week's blast

The emotional level that has been achieved
Wraps our arms around those who are bereaved

An incredible thing, a difficult feat
We've united against you; we are in no way beat!
9-21-01

Our Heroes

We know you are weary, we know you are worn
Experiencing so many emotions that leave you torn

Please hang in there and try not to get depressed
Their spirits are in heaven now among the best

They left us much too soon, we'd all agree
But it's not for us to decide how it will be

You'll carry the banner on behalf of your brothers
Continuing your work of helping others

God bless you one, God bless you all
You're always there to answer "The call!"
9-22-01

A Candle's Light

People are gathering everywhere
To lend support, to show they care

No more distinctions, no lines are drawn
Just humans uniting together as they mourn

It's really heartwarming, quite a sight
No language barriers in the glow of a candle's light

The human spirit is really quite strong
So movingly shown in spontaneous song!

America *is* beautiful
God bless America
9-23-01

Healing Our Spirit

Hard to believe it's two weeks ago today
That our country was violated this way

The pain delivered to us has been intense
The emotional toll has been immense

The president and the mayor ask for the healing to begin
A huge request, considering where we have all just been

Yes, there has been so much destruction
Lives forever changed with all this disruption

If we don't move forward, then they have won
We will rise victorious, regardless of what they have done

Oh, we hurt, of that there is no doubt
But being resilient is what we are about

We can't function if we are consumed by grief
Healing will start giving us emotional relief

Our loved ones will not have died in vain
As long as we pick ourselves up and start again

All these souls are at peace in God's kingdom
We must trust in His infinite wisdom!
9-25-01

Terrible Images

Terrible images etched on our minds
Of this assault against all mankind

Yes, this happened on American soil
But the ripple effect touches us all

Everything has been documented since day one
Captured by photographers and citizens forced to run

They too were victims of the horrific blast
Who captured these visions guaranteed to last

So painful to watch; we ask ourselves how
We've all studied history, but this is now

It's our friends and family, people we know
We've been hurled to a spot none of us wants to go

Never believing this could happen here
Seeing our children react with fear

It's up to us now to do what needs to be done
So once again they can feel secure to play and run

If they thought they could divide us, they were oh so wrong
We have linked arms, and our resolve is forever strong!
9-26-01

Heartwarming

It's heartwarming seeing Old Glory flying proudly everywhere
From homes, buildings, and cars to show we care

It's something we've felt, but never felt the need to show
Now you can see our colors wherever you go

United regardless of faith, color, or creed
The human race bonded in this time of need!
9-26-01

They Will Not Stop!

These men are still working around the clock
Determined in their quest, they will not stop

Machinery working day and night
Hoping against hope they'll find someone all right

Silhouetted against the skyline, you see a large crane
Scooping up the rubble again and again

Now more bodies are being discovered
As the base of the buildings are being uncovered

Each one is handled with gentle respect
Knowing these men, it's what we've learned to expect

The men remove their hats and gather around
All in prayer, some kneeling on the ground

Then it's back to work they go
There is so much to do, this they know!
9-28-01

Can't Believe Their Eyes

Anyone visiting the site is shocked by what they see
This is New York City, not how it's supposed to be

Thousands of workers busy getting ready to start their day
Now lay in shambles, murdered in such a terrible way

The senselessness of it all rocks us to our very core
It's hit home now; we aren't innocents anymore

We'll find a way to work through this; it'll just take some time
But we've got to do it together to protect what's yours and mine!
10-2-01

Return to the City

Tourists now starting to return to the city
To see for themselves, although it's not pretty

A look of sadness crosses over their face
The Twin Towers are gone, destruction has taken it's place

But equally impressed by the courage they see
Everyone pulling together the way it should be

They know we are down but definitely not out
We're picking up the pieces, getting out and about

It's important to get into a daily routine
Though no one can forget the horrors they've seen!
10-3-01

The Sound of the Beepers

The sound of the beepers, only the fireman knows
A part of his equipment wherever he goes

A beeping sound, the flashing light
Enabling them to be found day or night

On September 11th what a mournful sound
So many beepers activated from under the ground

The pain and frustration these firemen must have felt
This is more destruction than any of us have ever been dealt

In their hearts, they knew it was already too late
There is no way to understand the hands of fate

Please just remember all the lives that you did save
From this monster that is totally depraved

Because of you, they live to face another day
And no words are adequate to thank you, they would say

Your brothers need you to carry on in their honor too
Because they are your brothers, that's exactly what you'll do

They will never be forgotten by family or friends
They may be out of sight, but it's not where it ends

They'll live on in the memory of those they've touched
A part of all who loved them so much!
10-04-01

Closure

So much attention, so much exposure
It's difficult trying to find some kind of closure

How do you accept what you cannot see?
This is not the way it's supposed to be

When a loved one dies, you hold a wake
We can't do this and it's hard to take

Our hearts cry out for just one more glance
Because of terrible times, we'll never get that chance

Our minds know what our hearts can't believe
But we are not alone now as we grieve

It's a date we all have in common—September 11
Our faith teaches us they are now at peace in heaven!
10-4-01

America Strikes Back

We've bombed Afghanistan at their military bases
We try to avoid killing civilians in all cases

This is only our first military action
America striking back at their terrorist faction

We are not a nation to mess with lightly
We hold on to our freedoms very tightly

The lines are drawn, they will not negotiate
This is what happens when people are consumed with hate

Those who support terrorism will fall in defeat
We will not stand for it, they will feel our heat

We have now attacked them where they live
Not one more inch are we willing to give

This will be a difficult campaign
This is not the easiest terrain

Now it has started, now it's begun
America strikes back; they are on the run!
10-7-01

Doing Our Part

Every American must play a part
Due to this tragedy that has touched our heart

You hear about acts of generosity every day
Trying to help each other is the American way

Kids donated money that they saved for a trip
In the spirit of sharing, they have quite a grip

Stars and TV shows donated their proceeds
To ensure those in need will be able to succeed

Stores have donated their profits from a sale
Working together in this spirit, we just can't fail!
10-8-01

Taking Control of Our Lives

Listening on the news that a hijacking was aborted
Passengers are acting swiftly now, it has been reported

Believing he was saving the Sears Tower was a mentally ill man
Who, in his own mind, was doing the best that he can

A sad situation that left everyone scared
But sending a message that civilians are prepared

If it were a terrorist, this is something they need to know
There is more of us than there is of them—a unity we now show

We won't let them harm us; we will take back control
They'll never know which of us is an air marshal on patrol!
10-9-01

In a Hostile Land

Our military now fighting in a hostile land
A war that we can all understand

They are fighting for our freedom from fear
They are fighting for all the rights we hold dear

It's hard for them being so far from home
I'm sure they are scared and feeling alone

We pray for the safety of all of them there
We are proud of them all; we hope they are aware!
10-13-01

Memorials

We went to Eagle Rock Reservation today
And what we saw would take your breath away

Makeshift memorials were everywhere
A way to show how much we care

American flags, candles, poems, and pictures
Different ways of showing grief, it's quite a mixture

We look out over the New York skyline and see an empty space
The view from this New Jersey spot has become a reflecting place

A quiet spot to come and grieve
And say heartfelt prayers before we leave!
10-15-01

Souls to Paradise

Leading funeral processions for their brothers in blue
Piping their souls into paradise, it's what they do

This has been a long-standing tradition
Familiar tunes in a bagpiper's rendition

A sea of blue standing side by side
Saluting their comrades while tears they try to hide

So many funerals at once is not the norm
The magnitude of it all must leave them forlorn

This is a tragedy that has left us all reeling
But as Americans, we will find a way of dealing!
10-16-01

Now It's Anthrax

Now they are attacking us with deadly anthrax
These cowards always strike behind our backs

Why do they feel the need to kill?
Or making innocent people desperately ill?

With terroristic attacks, what do they have to gain?
With a mentality like theirs, it's impossible to explain

They have absolutely no regard for human decency
And when they are caught, they will get no leniency!
10-17-01

A Story of Hope

You turn on the TV, all the news is bad
All this tragedy, it makes us feel sad

Then something happens that makes you smile
A cat and her kittens were buried for quite a while

Trapped in the basement, she must have been scared
How can we explain why they were spared?

In a box full of napkins, three little kittens were born
A story of hope as the nation mourns

So naming the mother Hope seems only natural
Other patriotic names will help keep things factual

So the kittens are named Freedom, Amber, and Flag
Doing what kittens do—eat, sleep, romp, and play tag!
10-17-01

Speculation

Speculation has started; what to do?
There is sure to be many a point of view

Because of this void in the sky
What can we do so their memory won't die?

Do we rebuild the Twin Towers proud and tall?
That could be painful to those who watched them fall

Do we build a monument on this site?
It's a difficult decision; we want to do what is right

We are forging on; our healing has begun
Only time now will tell what will be done!
10-21-01

Anthrax Hoax

Why would these people stage a hoax?
What would make them think that this is a joke?

Do they think it's funny to spread such fears?
Does it give them a thrill to see people in tears?

It's bad enough people are sick from the real anthrax
That our people would do; this is despicable and that's a fact

It's the full extent of the law, when caught, that they will feel
We won't take this lightly; it's much too real!
10-23-01

Dissension

It's been a long time; emotions are raw
Everyone is saddened by what they saw

Firemen and policemen squared off at ground zero
A dispute about recovering our fallen heroes

The mayor now feels it's getting more dangerous at the site
And wants to drastically reduce those working throughout the night

He doesn't want a collapse and more loss of life
Different thoughts about this is causing strife

More bodies are being recovered now after working so hard
This is closure for them, and now they are being barred

The authorities want machines to go in and remove the debris
To sort somewhere else, wherever that might be

It doesn't seem right, it doesn't seem fair
Human remains must be treated with dignity and care!
11-3-01

More Tragedy

Another plane has fallen from the sky
More speculation now and we're asking why

It had departed the airport JFK
Terror strikes our hearts again in a terrible way

No one knows yet if it's a terrorist's attack
Or just some horrible accident; we have no facts

It's just two months and one day since our world fell apart
No wonder we react to this with a broken heart

Regardless of the results, though, there has been loss of life
Just as we were learning to live among all this strife!
11-12-01

Three Minutes

(American Airlines flight 587 departing to Santo Domingo)

9:14 AM to 9:17 AM is only three minutes of time
What a change this can make in life, both yours and mine

Happy excitement at the thought of a trip
On airport radar, it was just another blip

People on the ground so safe in their home
Starting their day as usual, who could have known?

Business as usual is what we've been trying to do
Now something else rocks the world of me and you

Since 9-11-01, we've had so much destruction and pain
Will we ever know what "normal" is ever again?
11-12-01

Casualties of War

"They were the casualties of a war" is what he said
A man whose son and comrades now lay dead

Victims of the terrorist's attack on New York City
A statement of fact, he wasn't looking for pity

The pain was apparent in his eyes and on his face
Such loss of life, it's a terrible waste

When you look at it like that, it really is true
A war has been declared against me and you

They attacked us at home where we work and live
And shook our way of life which we would never give

It was meant to hurt us and tear us apart
But instead, united us into one huge American heart!
11-14-01

73 Days and Nights

Since the disaster, it's been seventy-three days and nights
And now we're at war to protect our rights

Time has passed quickly, and now it's Thanksgiving Day
And we're busy with our traditions; it's the American way

This year's New York's Macy's parade had a patriotic theme
With a great deal of emotion, that's how it seemed

Two huge flags were carried side by side
Symbols of our Twin Towers carried with pride

Memories of lost loved ones brought many tears
Remembering Thanksgivings of previous years

But so proud of how this country has pulled together
Because our spirits are as strong as ever!
11-22-01

Internal Wounds

Internal wounds too deep to see
By the tragedy that befell on you and me

So much pain and so much grief
Only the gift of time can bring some relief

These daily problems were unknown before now
Who would have thought this could happen anyhow?

Family structures have changed because of death
Trying to cope, almost impossible for those who are bereft

That's why the rest of us must step in with a helping hand
To offer support and to show that we understand!
11-27-01

Another Soul Found at the Twin Towers

Another body was discovered today from underground
In silent prayer, everyone gathered around

I'm sure everyone who's lost someone is praying it's theirs
This flag-draped soul is the answer to someone's prayer

Perhaps more will be found that will help families heal
From this horror that is so deep and so real!
12-6-01

Images

These images they show us are as chilling as it can get
Photos and written accounts so that we will never forget

Some of us lost loved ones; our lives are forever changed
For others, it's our way of life that has been rearranged

Now our military troops are at risk, fighting in Afghanistan
Just as our fathers had done before fighting in a foreign land

The holidays are quickly approaching; we try hard to hide our tears
Extremely difficult as it won't be the same as it was in previous years

It's exactly three months ago today that our loved ones were taken away
Not for one second do we forget as we bow our heads and pray

Remember that as long as they are in our hearts, they are never far away
And to honor their memories, together we will face another day!
12-11-01

Cycle of Violence

"A cycle of violence," an effective term
And the destruction it brings, won't we ever learn?

I hurt yours, then you hurt mine
It's so inhumane, it crosses the line

Granted we can't let it happen, we must retaliate
But when did it start, this consuming hate?

Why do they hate us because we are Americans?
In destroying innocents, they'll do anything they can

They have started something we are forced to finish
Try as they might, our spirit will never diminish!
12-12-01

The Smoking Gun!

This is what we needed—"the smoking gun"
Absolute proof Osama bin Laden is the guilty one

A damning witness against himself, this monster of death
Buying terror and destruction with his immense wealth

No doubt will be left in anyone's mind
This video of his conversation was quite a find

It's chilling as we listen to him laugh and boast
At the number of deaths he caused thrilled him the most

He praises Allah for what he has done
His total disregard for life, he's truly the evil one

This coward is on the run, hiding in caves under the ground
But count on this: we won't stop until this vermin has been found!
12-13-01

The Flame Has Burned Out

One hundred days since 9-11-01, and the flame finally burned out
The outrage of it all still makes us want to shout

Ground zero had continued to simmer and smolder
A constant reminder of our loved ones who will never grow older

So senseless and unwarranted was this early-morning attack
A very hard lesson that now we must always watch our back

Bin Laden, the coward that he is, is still on the run
Now has a huge reward on his head, this evil one

It won't be long before he is turned over to us
Like the others, he'll be a crybaby who kicks up a fuss

His style is to sneak up behind our backs
Then run and hide after the attacks

We have all grown as a nation, and we will always stand tall
Regardless of what he tried to do, we will never fall!
12-20-01

The Holidays

This has been such an incredible year
It's imperative for the kids that we show some cheer

It's difficult to do with a heavy heart
But for the sake of the kids, we must do our part

We learn that no matter what happens to us, life still moves on
Going forward even when mourning those who have gone

We all need the feeling that our structure is intact
There's security in tradition and that's a fact

You'll find that by reassuring them, you actually reassure yourself
Take a deep breath, smile, and forge ahead as Santa's elf!
12-22-01

The Year 2001

The year 2001 has been tragic but unique
Meaning different things to whomever you speak

We won't let what has happened to us make us run for cover
So many good things have happened too, with more to discover

The "evil one" is still playing hide-and-seek
In his vast hideaways in the mountains so deep

It's only time before he runs out of places to go
Eventually we will uncover him, this we know

Who knows if we'll get him alive or dead
But there certainly is a big-enough bounty on his head

Let's look forward with hope in our hearts to the year 2002
This is a brand-new slate for me and you

As Americans, we are strong and resilient
We will protect our homeland that is beautiful and brilliant!
12-28-01

Observation Platform

They are opening the observation platform to see ground zero
A place for us to visit and pray over our fallen heroes

It will hold up to four hundred people and the height is thirteen feet
Located in Lower Manhattan at Fulton and Church streets

Seeing with your own eyes, it becomes part of the healing process
And to witness the action of cleanup may help ease our distress

This is a place to come to so we can pause and reflect
To honor all who died here and to show our respect!
12-29-01

Health Problems

New problems surface from the 9-11 attack
This is a tough one for us to fight back

Rescuers and workers at the site are now getting ill
Another horror thrust upon us against our will

Clouds of glass and concrete dust invaded their lungs
This threat of long-term danger has just begun

Shortness of breath, dry cough, affecting one out of four
Dizziness and feelings of drowning, I'm sure that there's more

High levels of mercury in the blood are now being found
Who knows what else was kicked up as everything crashed to the ground

One more insult aside from losing colleagues and friends
What else will crop up, will this suffering ever end?
1-8-02

We have been dealt a terrible blow
We will survive it, this we know
Our human spirit is proud and strong
"God Bless America" has become our national song!

There is no end to this book;
it's actually only the beginning because
new stories emerge daily.
There are and will continue to be stories
and situations that will touch the entire spectrum
of human emotions.

Edwards Brothers, Inc.
Thorofare, NJ USA
October 5, 2011